Great Hymns

Instrumental Solos for Worship

Arranged by James Curnow

Contents

5 ALL CREATURES OF OUR GOD AND KING
6 PRAISE TO THE LORD, THE ALMIGHTY
7 BE THOU MY VISION
8 O WORSHIP THE KING
9 JOYFUL, JOYFUL, WE ADORE THEE
10 BRETHREN, WE HAVE MET TO WORSHIP
11 WE GATHER TOGETHER
12 I SING THE MIGHTY POWER OF GOD
13 A MIGHTY FORTRESS IS OUR GOD
14 ALL HAIL THE POWER

To access audio, visit:
www.halleonard.com/mylibrary

Enter Code
6261-3613-9106-0871

ISBN 978-90-431-0981-9

Exclusively Distributed By
HAL•LEONARD®

Visit Hal Leonard Online at
www.halleonard.com

Contact us:
Hal Leonard
7777 West Bluemound Road
Milwaukee, WI 53213
Email: info@halleonard.com

In Europe, contact:
Hal Leonard Europe Limited
42 Wigmore Street
Marylebone, London, W1U 2RN
Email: info@halleonardeurope.com

In Australia, contact:
Hal Leonard Australia Pty. Ltd.
4 Lentara Court
Cheltenham, Victoria, 3192 Australia
Email: info@halleonard.com.au

Great Hymns

INTRODUCTION

This collection of some of the world's greatest hymns was created for, and is dedicated to, my good friend and musical colleague, Philip Smith, Principal Trumpet, New York Philharmonic Orchestra. The goal of these arrangements is to allow instrumentalists the opportunity to give praise and adoration to God through their musical abilities.

Though the arrangements have been written for trumpet, with Phil in mind, cued notes have been added to allow players at many different levels and on various instruments to perform them. They are also playable on all instruments (C treble clef, Bb Treble Clef, Eb, F or Bass Clef) by simply purchasing the appropriate book that coincides with the key of their instrument.

The piano accompaniment book has been written to work with all instruments; an accompaniment track for each hymn is also included with the online audio, should a piano accompanist not be available. Appropriate tuning notes have also been included to allow soloists the opportunity to adjust their intonation to the intonation of the audio.

May you enjoy using this collection and find it useful in extending your musical ministry.

Kindest regards,

James Curnow
President
Curnow Music Press, Inc.

Audio performed by Becky Shaw - Piano, Michael Rintamaa - Organ, Phil Smith - Trumpet

PHILIP SMITH

Principal trumpet

NEW YORK PHILHARMONIC

Philip Smith joined the New York Philharmonic as Co-Principal Trumpet in October 1978, and became Principal Trumpet in June 1988. His early training was provided at The Salvation Army, and continued under the training of his father, Derek Smith. He is a graduate of The Julliard School, having studied with Edward Treutel and William Vacchiano. In January of 1975, while still at Juilliard, Mr. Smith was appointed to the Chicago Symphony Orchestra by Sir Georg Solti.

Mr. Smith has appeared regularly as soloist, recitalist, chamber orchestra performer and clinician. He has been featured as a soloist with the Philharmonic in over 75 performances under such conductors as Zubin Mehta, Kurt Masur, Erich Leinsdorf, Leonard Bernstein, and Neeme Jarvi. Highlights have included the World Premiere of Joseph Turrin's Concerto with the New York Philharmonic, its subsequent European Premiere with the Leipzig Gewandhaus Orchestra, the U.S. Premiere of Jacques Hetu's Concerto, and an upcoming World Premiere of Lowell Liebermano's Concerto. He has been a guest soloist with the Edmonton Symphony, Newfoundland Symphony, Columbus (IN) Symphony, Pensacola (FL) Symphony, Hartford (CT) Symphony, and Beaumont (TX) Symphony.

Mr. Smith has also appeared with many symphonic wind ensembles including La Philharmonic des Vents des Quebec, the Hanover Wind Symphony, the Ridgewood Concert Band, and many major university wind ensembles. Most recently he appeared at The College Band Directors National Association Convention in Austin, Texas for the World Premiere of Turrin's *Chronicles* with the University of New Mexico Wind Ensemble.

An avid brass band enthusiast, Mr. Smith has been guest soloist with the US Army Brass Band, Goteborg Brass (Sweden), Black Dyke Mills (Britain), Hannaford Silver Band and Intrada Brass (Canada), and numerous American and Salvation Army Brass Bands. A particular highlight was appearing as featured soloist at the 1996 British Open Brass Band Championships in Manchester, England.

Mr. Smith is on the faculty at The Juilliard School and has appeared as recitalist and clinician at the Grand Teton Music Festival, Swiss Brass Week, Breman (Germany) Trumpet Days, Oslo (Finland) Trumpet Week, Harmony Ridge (VT) Festival, Scotia Festival of Music and numerous International Trumpet Guild conferences, most recently in Goteborg, Sweden in 1997.

Mr. Smith has performed and recorded with the Canadian Brass, the Empire Brass, Chamber Music Society of Lincoln Center, Mostly Mozart Orchestra, Bargemusic and NY Virtuosi Chamber Symphony. His solo recordings include Copeland's *Quiet City* (Deutsche Grammophone), *New York Legend* (CALA Records), *Orchestral Excerpts for Trumpet* (Summit Records), Ellen Taaffe Zwilich's *Concerto for Trumpet and Five Instruments* (New World Records), Bach's *Brandenburg Concerto No. 2* (Koch Records), Walton's *Façade* (Arabesque Records), and *The Trump Shall Resound* and *Repeat the Sounding Joy* (Heritage Records/Resounding Praise). Two new projects will be released in the spring of 2000; a solo CD with The Salvation Army New York Staff Band, and CD and music arrangements entitled Great Hymns published by Curnow Music Press.

Mr. Smith lives in New Jersey with his wife Sheila, teaches Bible Study at the Montclair Salvation Army, and gives all praise and honor to the Lord God Almighty.

P.O. Box 142, Wilmore, KY 40390, USA
Edition Number: CMP 0357.00

Copyright © 2000 by Curnow Music Press, Inc.

Dedicated to Philip Smith, Principal Trumpet, New York Philharmonic Orchestra

BE THOU MY VISION

Slane

Arr. **James Curnow** (ASCAP)

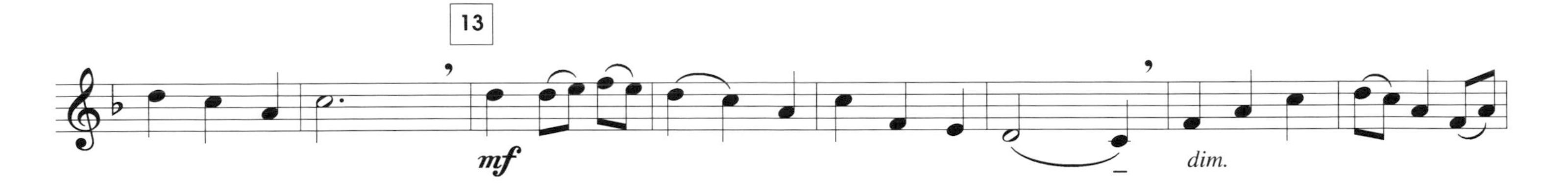

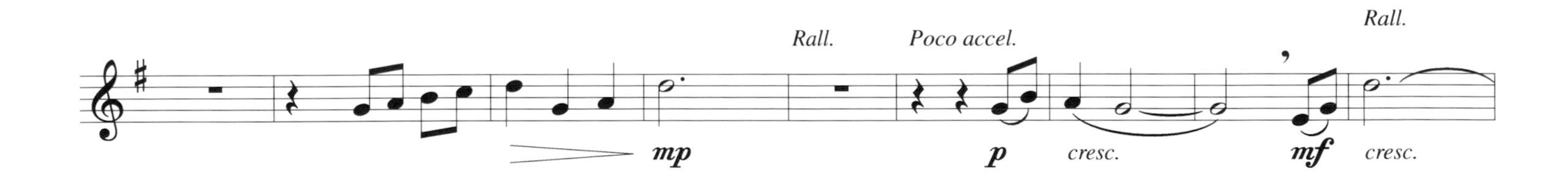

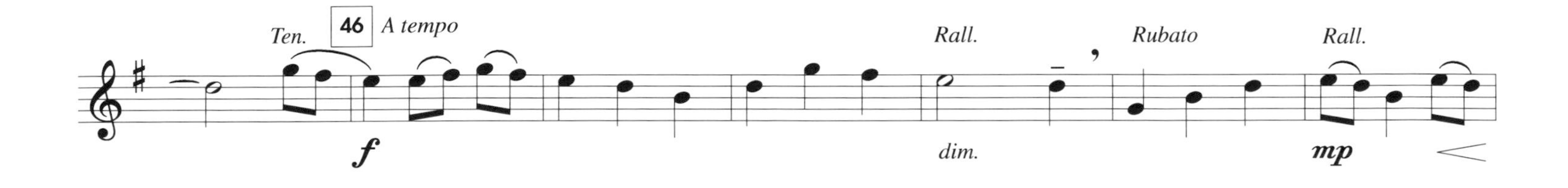

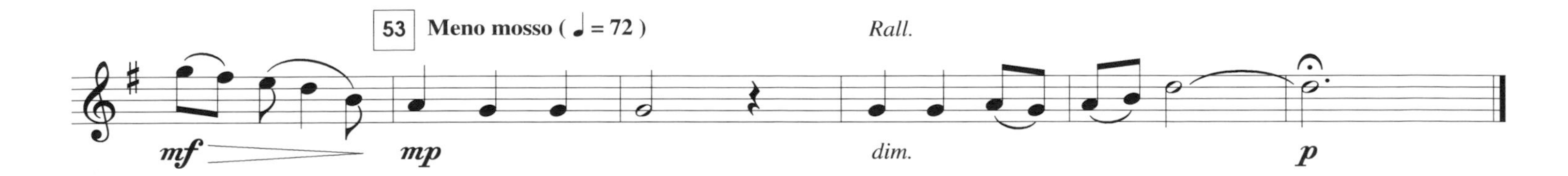

Dedicated to Philip Smith, Principal Trumpet, New York Philharmonic Orchestra

O WORSHIP THE KING

Lyons

Arr. **James Curnow** (ASCAP)

Dedicated to Philip Smith, Principal Trumpet, New York Philharmonic Orchestra

JOYFUL, JOYFUL, WE ADORE THEE

Hymn to Joy

Arr. **James Curnow** (ASCAP)

Dedicated to Philip Smith, Principal Trumpet, New York Philharmonic Orchestra
BRETHREN, WE HAVE MET TO WORSHIP
Holy Manna Variations
Arr. James Curnow (ASCAP)
Religioso, espresivo (♩ = 84)
(Trumpet to optional Flugelhorn)
legato
p – mp
mf
Rall.
A tempo
mp
Rall.
Piu mosso (♩ = 100)
(Optional Flugelhorn to Trumpet)
p
mf
f
1.
2.
Rall.
Adagio (♩ = 72)
(Trumpet to optional Flugelhorn)
cresc.
A tempo
cresc.
Rall.
Poco meno mosso
(Optional Flugelhorn to Trumpet)
Allegro moderato (♩ = 126)
mp cresc.
mf marc.
dim.
Moderately slow (♩ = 76)
legato
Meno mosso
ff

Dedicated to Philip Smith, Principal Trumpet, New York Philharmonic Orchestra
WE GATHER TOGETHER
Kremser
Arr. James Curnow (ASCAP)
Maestoso (♩ = 100)
Optional 8va
f marc.
Rall.
A tempo
ff
mp legato
cresc.
mf
mp
p
Rall.
cresc.
f
A tempo
mf
cresc.
f
mf
cresc.
f
cresc.
Rall.
ff

Dedicated to Philip Smith, Principal Trumpet, New York Philharmonic Orchestra
I SING THE MIGHTY POWER OF GOD
Ellacombe
Arr. James Curnow (ASCAP)
Allegro moderato con dignita (♩ = 116)
marc.
cresc.
(In a feeling of two)
legato
In four
Rall.
A tempo
cresc.
legato
marc.

Dedicated to Philip Smith, Principal Trumpet, New York Philharmonic Orchestra
A MIGHTY FORTRESS IS OUR GOD
Ein' Feste Burg
Arr. James Curnow (ASCAP)
Allegro maestoso (♩ = 112)
3
5
f marc.
Rall.
11
A tempo
mf
19
Meno mosso (♩ = 92)
Rall.
30
8
38
Rall.
Meno mosso (♩ = 88)
mp legato
cresc.
f
3
Rall.
48
Andante maestoso (♩ = 84)
mf legato
Rall.
mp
Meno mosso (♩ = 82)
p
Rall.
marc.
58
A tempo (♩ = 82)
f
Rall.
tr
mf
A tempo
legato
64
(Optional 8va to m. 68)
marc.
Rall.
Meno mosso (♩ = 80)
f
Rall.
69
Trionfale (♩ = 96)
ff
2
Rall.

Dedicated to Philip Smith, Principal Trumpet, New York Philharmonic Orchestra
ALL HAIL THE POWER
Coronation, Diadem, Miles Lane
Arr. James Curnow (ASCAP)
Allergro moderato e maestoso (♩ = 112)
marc.
cresc.
Rall.
A tempo (♩ = 112)
cresc.
Rall.
A tempo
Rall.
Adagio moderato espressivo (♩ = 88)
legato
Poco accel.
Rall.
Tempo primo (♩ = 112)
cresc. e marc.
Rall.
A tempo
(Optional 8va
(8va)
Rall.
cresc.

ALSO AVAILABLE

More Great Hymns

Instrumental Solos for Worship

Arranged by James Curnow

This collection of some of the world's greatest hymns was created for, and is dedicated to Philip Smith, Principal Trumpet, New York Philharmonic Orchestra. They are delightfully arranged in fresh settings by some of the foremost arrangers in the instrumental field. The accompaniment CD (included in the solo book) provides a demonstration performance of each solo by Phil Smith. It also allows the soloist to practice or perform with the CD when an accompanist is not available. May you enjoy using this collection and find it useful in extending your musical ministry.

Contents: *How Firm A Foundation* • *Amazing Grace* • *Softly and Tenderly* • *O For A Thousand Tongues To Sing* • *Jesu, Joy of Man's Desiring* • *Holy God, We Praise Thy Name* • *Easter Glory* • *Holy, Holy, Holy* • *Lead On, O King Eternal* • *My Faith Looks Up To Thee*